CONTENTS

Handa's Surprise
by Eileen Browne

INTRODUCTION
Handa's Surprise by Eileen Browne — 3

WAYS IN
Introducing the story — 4

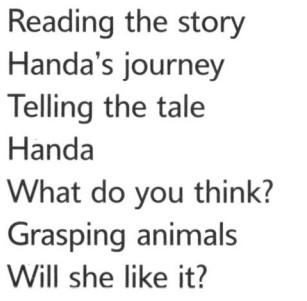

MAKING SENSE
Reading the story — 5
Handa's journey — 6
Telling the tale — 6
Handa — 8
What do you think? — 9
Grasping animals — 9
Will she like it? — 12
Fruit salad — 13
Vanishing fruit — 13
Fruit basket game — 16
African animals — 16
Village life — 20

DEVELOPING IDEAS
Puppet play — 22
Another surprise! — 22
A present for Handa — 25
Thank you for the surprise! — 25
Other animals — 27
Handa's story — 27
Lift the flap — 28

EVALUATION
Meeting time — 30

HELP!
Using this book — 31

CREDITS

Published by Scholastic Ltd,
Villiers House,
Clarendon Avenue,
Leamington Spa,
Warwickshire CV32 5PR
Text © Guy Merchant
© 2000 Scholastic Ltd
2 3 4 5 6 7 8 9 0   1 2 3 4 5 6 7 8 9

Author Guy Merchant
Editor Irene Goodacre
Series designer Lynne Joesbury
Illustrations Eileen Browne
Cover illustration Eileen Browne

Designed using Adobe Pagemaker

British Library Cataloguing-in-Publication Data
A catalogue record for this book is available from the British Library.

ISBN 0-590-53984-1

The right of Guy Merchant to be identified as the Author of this work has been asserted by him in accordance with the Copyright, Designs and Patents Act 1988.

All rights reserved. This book is sold subject to the condition that it shall not, by way of trade or otherwise, be lent, hired out or otherwise circulated without the publisher's prior consent in any form of binding or cover other than that in which it is published and without a similar condition, including this condition, being imposed upon the subsequent purchaser.

No part of this publication may be reproduced, stored in a retrieval system, or transmitted, in any form or by any means, electronic, mechanical, photocopying, recording or otherwise, without the prior permission of the publisher. This book remains copyright, although permission is granted to copy pages 4 to 30 for classroom distribution and use only in the school which has purchased the book and in accordance with the CLA licensing agreement. Photocopying permission is given for purchasers only and not for borrowers of books from any lending service.

ACKNOWLEDGEMENTS

Walker Books Limited, London for the use of text and illustrations from *Handa's Surprise* by Eileen Browne © 1994, Eileen Browne (1994, Walker).
Ruth Atkinson, Debbie Goodwin and the children from Digby C of E School, Lincoln.

INTRODUCTION

Handa's Surprise
by Eileen Browne

What's the plot of the story?
Handa chooses seven different fruits as a gift for her friend Akeyo. She loads them into a basket and carries them on her head as she walks to Akeyo's village. On the way they are taken, one by one, by animals from the game reserve, although Handa cannot see this happening. Handa's basket is completely empty when a tethered goat breaks free and crashes into a tangerine tree, spilling the fresh fruit into Handa's basket. When Handa meets Akeyo she is as surprised as her friend to learn that her basket is now full of tangerines. Fortunately they are Akeyo's favourite fruit!

What's so good about this book?
This is a brilliantly conceived picture book in which the pictures work together with the written text to tell the story. The illustrations are bright and warm, giving us a feel for life in Kenya. Handa's character is carefully drawn and developed – her kindness and resourcefulness as she fills the basket, balancing it on a bucket so that it is easier to pick up and put on her head; her concern as the basket gets lighter; her worry as she senses the larger animals approaching; her relief when she sees Akeyo and, finally, their shared surprise. The story has predictable and patterned language features.

Handa cannot see what is going on because the basket is balanced on her head. The written text follows her thoughts, while the visual text tells us another story. *Handa's Surprise* is set on a game reserve in Kenya, and gives an authentic representation of a Luo tribal village.

About Eileen Browne
Eileen Browne was born in Birmingham. She worked as a teacher in London and produced her first picture book in 1977. She now lives in Wiltshire. Eileen spent some time researching *Handa's Surprise*, which started life as a wordless picture book. She has tried to capture the essence of life on a game reserve in Kenya through the detail in the illustrations and her use of colour.

Her other books include *No Problem*, *Tick Tock* and *Where's That Bus?*. She has recently completed the artwork for *Footprints in the Forest: a Chembakolli Story*.

WAYS IN

Introducing the story

Learning intentions
- to make predictions about a book from its title and cover
- to learn about a book from the dedication
- to learn about the endpapers of a book

Organization
- whole class
- small pieces of different kinds of fruit (the fruits in the book will be available from most large supermarkets – include more familiar fruits if you wish)

Look at the front cover with the children. Ask them what the cover shows and what they think the story will be about. Draw their attention to the title and to the name of the author-illustrator. Ask:
- *How do you know which is which?*

Show the children the first and last pages of the book which have pictures of the fruit and the animals. Explain that both of these are called endpapers. (Suggest that they might include endpapers in books they write themselves.)

Turn to the first page of the story and ask the children to look closely at the illustration. Encourage them to look at the background and to think about where the story might be set.

Explain that sometimes an author writes a dedication that can tell us more about the story. Turn to the page and read the dedication aloud to the children. Ask if anyone knows where Kenya is, then explain that they will be finding out more about this later on.

Turn back to the endpaper that shows the fruit. Read out the names of the fruit one by one. Ask the children if they know what they taste like. End this introductory session by tasting the fruit. Encourage the children to talk about what the fruits look and taste like and, no doubt, their individual preferences!

Handa's Surprise — Read & Respond — Photocopiable

Reading the story

Learning intentions
- to become familiar with events in the story
- to predict events in the story using the pictures
- to introduce the idea of different points of view

Organization
- whole class

Begin by explaining that you are going to read the story with some pauses where you will ask questions. Read up to the point where Handa sets off to the village thinking 'I wonder which fruit she'll like best?'. Ask:
- *Which fruit do you think her friend will like best?*
- *Can you remember what it is called?*
- *What do you think might happen next?*

Continue to read until the antelope takes the avocado. Pause and ask:

- *What is happening to Handa's basket of fruit?*
- *Can she see what is happening?*
- *Do you think she knows what is happening... why?*
- *What is going to happen to the passion-fruit?*

Carry on reading (you will need to add in 'Will she like...' before 'the creamy green avocado' to preserve the meaning). Stop at the double page where the goat butts the tangerine tree. Ask the children to look carefully at each frame and describe to you what happens.
- *What do you think makes the goat break free?*
- *Why does it crash into the tree?* (You need to look carefully to notice how its front legs get caught in the rope.)

Read to the end of the book.
- *What was the surprise for Akeyo?*
- *Why was Handa surprised?*

Ask the children if they enjoyed the story. What was their favourite part?

Photocopiable   Handa's Surprise

MAKING SENSE

Handa's journey

Learning intentions
- to recall the events from the story in sequence
- to record the sequence of events with pictures
- to distinguish the beginning, middle and end of a story

Organization
- small group

Provide each group with a sheet of A3 paper (or larger) and ask the children to draw a line to represent the path of Handa's journey, with her own village at one end and Akeyo's village at the other. Suggest that they produce 'map-like' drawings of the villages and sketches of each incident that happens between one village and the other. (You may need to model this activity first with the whole class.) Encourage the children to label their diagrams, but don't insist on accurate spelling for all children.

Extension
Encourage the children to retell the events from their story maps. This can be practised as an independent activity and is ideal for presentation during the plenary session.

Telling the tale

Learning intentions
- to recall events from the story
- to put events in sequence
- to retell the story orally

Organization
- small group
- photocopiable page 7 (cut and laminated)
- tape recorder

Ask the children to use the pictures of fruits in the basket to sequence the narrative. These could simply be laid out in order on the carpet or pegged to a line with clothes pegs. Children then take turns to retell the story orally, using the pictures to help them. The story could be recorded on tape and played back to the whole class.

Extension
The story can be retold to the class during the plenary session. Children could use copies of the pictures of the basket on page 7 to make a simple comic strip of the story. These pictures should be displayed in the right order.

Handa's Surprise — *READ & RESPOND* — Photocopiable

Telling the tale

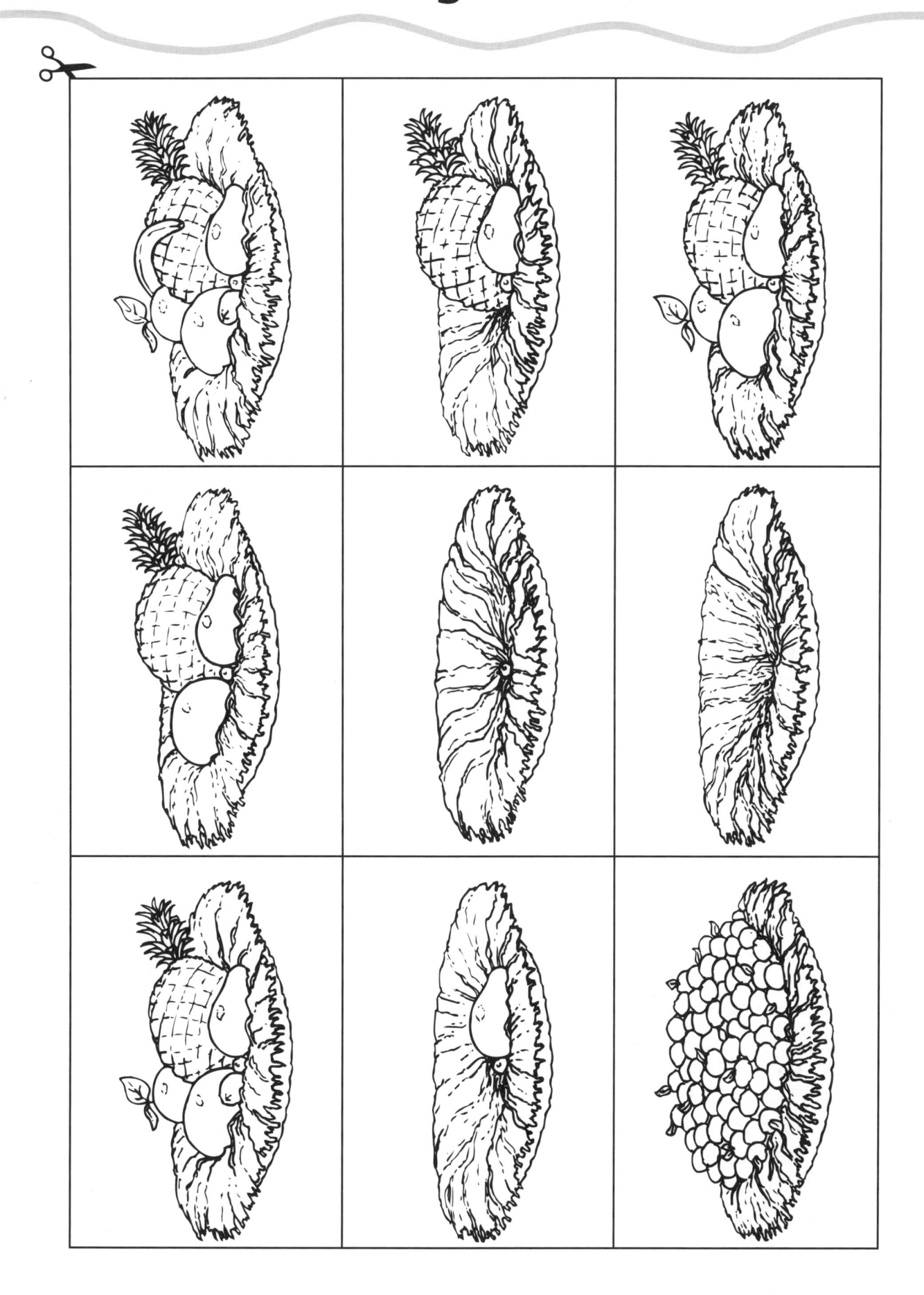

Handa's Surprise

Handda

Learning intentions
- to describe a character using the story and illustrations
- to understand a character's emotions and point of view

Organization
- whole class
- an outline figure of Handa drawn on a large sheet of paper
- a bank of words that describe Handa and her feelings, such as: frightened, excited, plaited hair, pink dress, happy, flip-flops, pleased, relieved, surprised

Before you work on this activity prepare a large outline of Handa, possibly by drawing around one of the children in your class (detail isn't important). Make sure you leave plenty of space on the paper around the outside of the figure. Pin this outline onto the wall.

Tell the children that they are going to help you write words and phrases that describe Handa. Words that describe what she looks like and what she does will be written outside the figure; words that describe what she thinks and feels will be written inside the figure.

Begin by looking at the third page of the story, the one that shows Handa setting off on her journey. Ask the children:
- *What can you tell me about Handa?*
- *How would you describe her to someone who has never read the book?* (She is black, her hair is braided, she wears flip-flops, she lives in a village in Kenya, and so on.)

Descriptions like these can be written around the outside of the figure.

Now encourage them to think about how she feels at the beginning of the story (excited about seeing Akeyo, pleased that she has so much fruit); how she feels in the middle (worried, upset, frightened) and how she feels at the end of the story (relieved, happy to see Akeyo, surprised to see the tangerines, puzzled about what has happened to the other fruit). The children may think of other words to describe Handa: she is kind, generous and brave. These ideas can be written inside the outline.

Look through the bank of words about Handa to see if you can match, or add to, the children's descriptions.

Extension
Children might write descriptions of Handa using the words and phrases you have collected. This could be done as sentence-length captions, while more confident writers could write a letter from Akeyo, introducing Handa as a pen-pal. 'Let me tell you about my friend Handa...'

What do you think?

Learning intentions
- to identify key moments in the story
- to see the story from another point of view

Organization
- whole class
- photocopiable page 10
- large circles of white card for 'thought bubbles'

Make an enlarged copy of photocopiable page 10, cut out each image and laminate it. Attach the pictures to a magnetic board or white board with a magnetic strip or Blu-Tack.

Look at each image in turn and ask the children to imagine what the character or animal is thinking. For example, the first image might have Handa thinking: 'I bet Akeyo really likes oranges'; in the second the monkey might think: 'Cor! I don't half fancy a banana!' and in the third picture Handa might think: 'That's funny, I'm sure I heard a large animal moving through the grass'. Once you have discussed this fill in the 'thought bubbles' as a shared writing activity.

Extension
Let children write their own 'thought bubbles' and captions for the images on photocopiable page 10. The pictures could be cut out in advance so that children have to put them in the right sequence.

Grasping animals

Learning intentions
- to explore key events in the story
- to look closely at the illustrations

Organization
- small group
- photocopiable page 11
- Big Book version of *Handa's Surprise* (if available)

With the children, look at the illustrations and note how the different animals take the fruit. Do they use their paws, beaks or mouths? Use the sentence maker at the bottom of page 11 as a model for children to record their answers.

You might wish to use photocopies of the pictures of animals on page 15 and fruit on page 18 to support less confident children.

What do you think?

Handa's Surprise Photocopiable

Grasping animals

paw	beak
mouth	trunk
tongue	mouth
beak	The _____ took the _____ with its _____.

Photocopiable
Read & Respond
Handa's Surprise

Will she like it?

Learning intentions
- to explore the language patterns in the text
- to look at the question form
- to learn the use of the question mark and full stop

Organization
- whole class
- a wordbank of large cards with all the words from the question 'Will she like the round juicy orange or the ripe red mango?' plus an additional 'will' (with a lower case 'w') and the word 'She' (with a capital 's')
- separate cards with a full stop and a question mark

Attach the words, in random order, to the wall or a flip chart. Look at the pages in which the zebra takes the orange and the elephant takes the mango. Read the sentence together.

Draw children's attention to the three dots (indicating a slight pause) and the question mark. Model the way that the sentence can be read with a slight rising intonation. You might like to read it again in this way with the class.

Close the book and ask the children if they can remember the question they have just practised. Ask them to help you find the right words from the wordbank.

Now show the children how to make another question with words from the wordbank, perhaps 'Will she like the orange?'. See how many other questions you can make.

Next, show the children how to turn a question into a statement, such as: 'She will like the mango.' Point out the changes in punctuation and capitalization. Repeat this with different statements from the wordbank and then revise making questions.

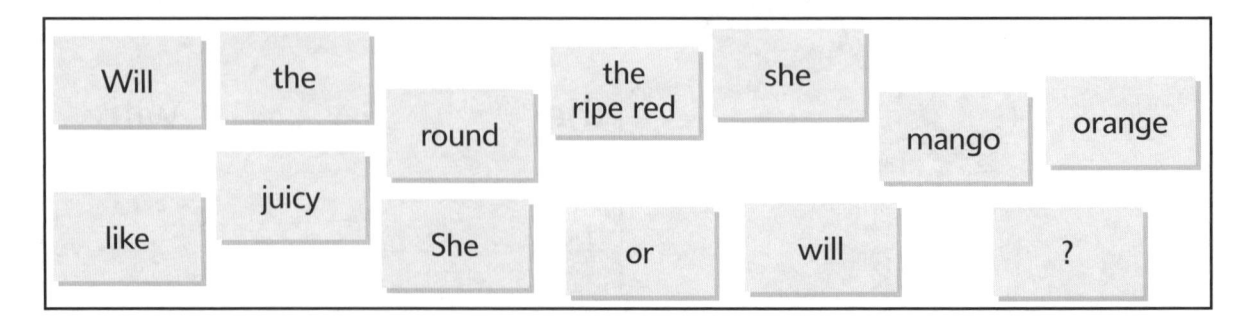

Will	the		the ripe red	she	
		round			mango	orange
like	juicy					
		She	or	will	?	

Handa's Surprise

Fruit salad

Learning intentions
- to read familiar words from the text
- to explore the use of descriptive words

Organization
- small group
- photocopiable page 14

Ask the children to cut out the pictures and words, then match the labels to the fruits. More confident readers will be able to do this without reference to the book; others may need the text for support.

Extension
Children can use the question starter 'Will she like the...' to make questions, using some or all of the fruits. You may need to remind them to add question marks after the fruit labels. These questions (with responses) could be stuck down and made into a group book: 'Will she like the soft yellow banana? No.'; 'Will she like the sweet-smelling guava?'; and so on, ending with 'Will she like the tangerines? YES!'

Vanishing fruit

Learning intentions
- to look closely at the illustrations
- to read and remember familiar words from the text
- to order words in a sentence

Organization
- small group
- photocopiable pages 14 and 15

Using photocopiable page 15, ask the children to match each fruit to the appropriate animal, then use the words from the labels on page 14 to make sentences, such as: 'The giraffe... picked up the... spiky-leaved pineapple.'

Fruit salad

● Cut out, then match, these words and pictures.

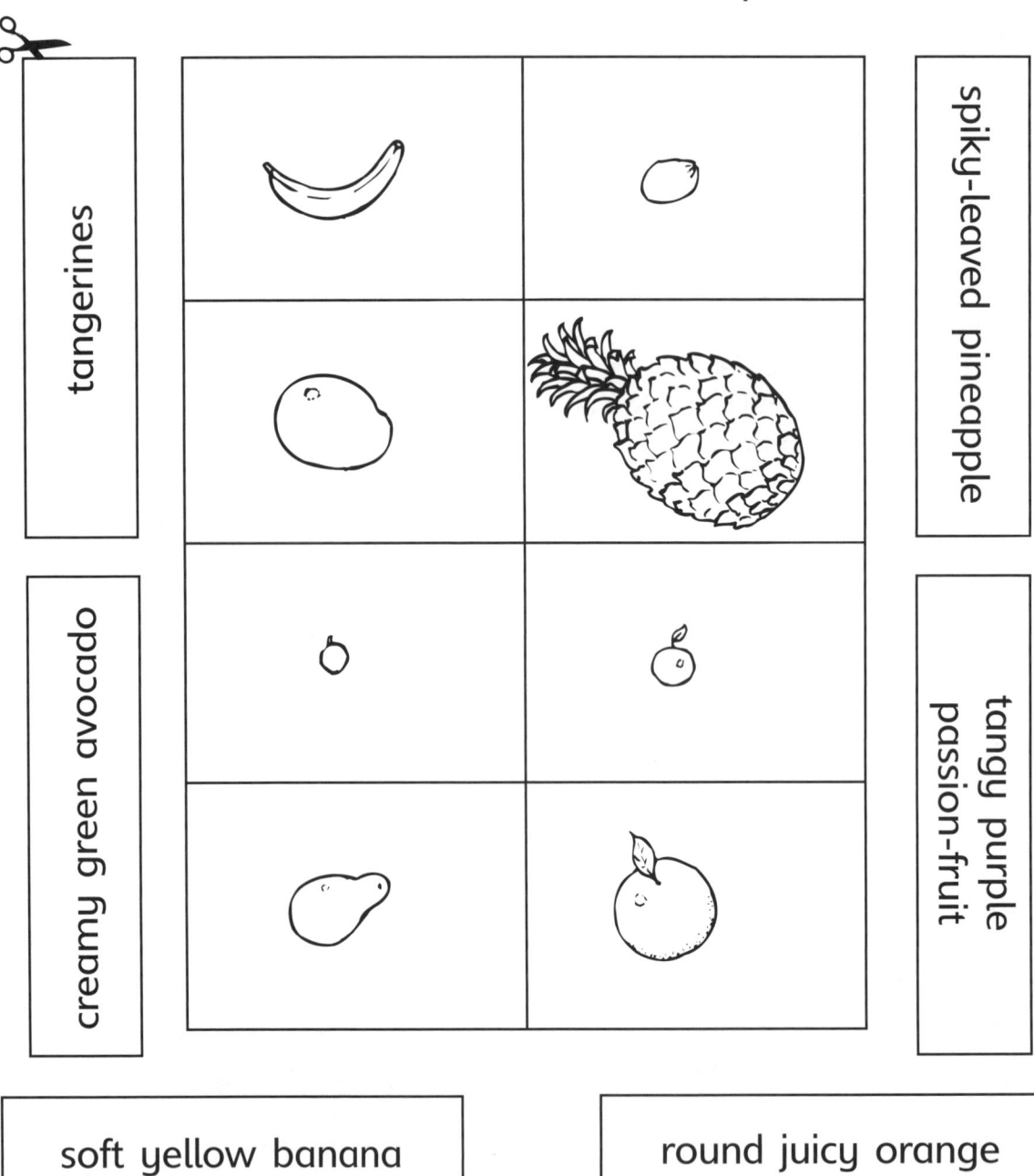

| tangerines | | | spiky-leaved pineapple |
| creamy green avocado | | | tangy purple passion-fruit |

soft yellow banana

round juicy orange

sweet-smelling guava

ripe red mango

Will she like the...

Handa's Surprise — Photocopiable

Vanishing fruit

ate the

Photocopiable

Handa's Surprise

Fruit basket game

Learning intentions
- to learn new sight vocabulary
- to explore concepts in the story

Organization
- small group
- photocopiable pages 17 and 18 (cut and laminated)
- fruit dice, made from the net on page 18

Give each child a basket with six empty fruit-shaped spaces (from page 17). Place the fruit shapes in the centre of the table. Tell the children to take turns to roll the dice and place the corresponding fruit in their basket. If that fruit is already in their basket then they miss a turn. The first child to fill his or her basket wins the game.

African animals

Learning intentions
- to learn new sight vocabulary
- to explore concepts in the story
- to use descriptive vocabulary

Organization
- small group
- photocopiable page 19

Ask the children to match one descriptive label to each animal.

Although the animals are not named in the text they are labelled on the endpapers if any children need support.

Extension
Ask the children to think of, and write, more descriptive words for each animal: perhaps the 'brown and yellow' giraffe. These can then be used to make a 'guess the animal' game for a plenary session. Simply fold a sheet of A4 paper lengthwise, then write the descriptive words on the outside and the animal name on the inside.

Handa's Surprise

Fruit basket

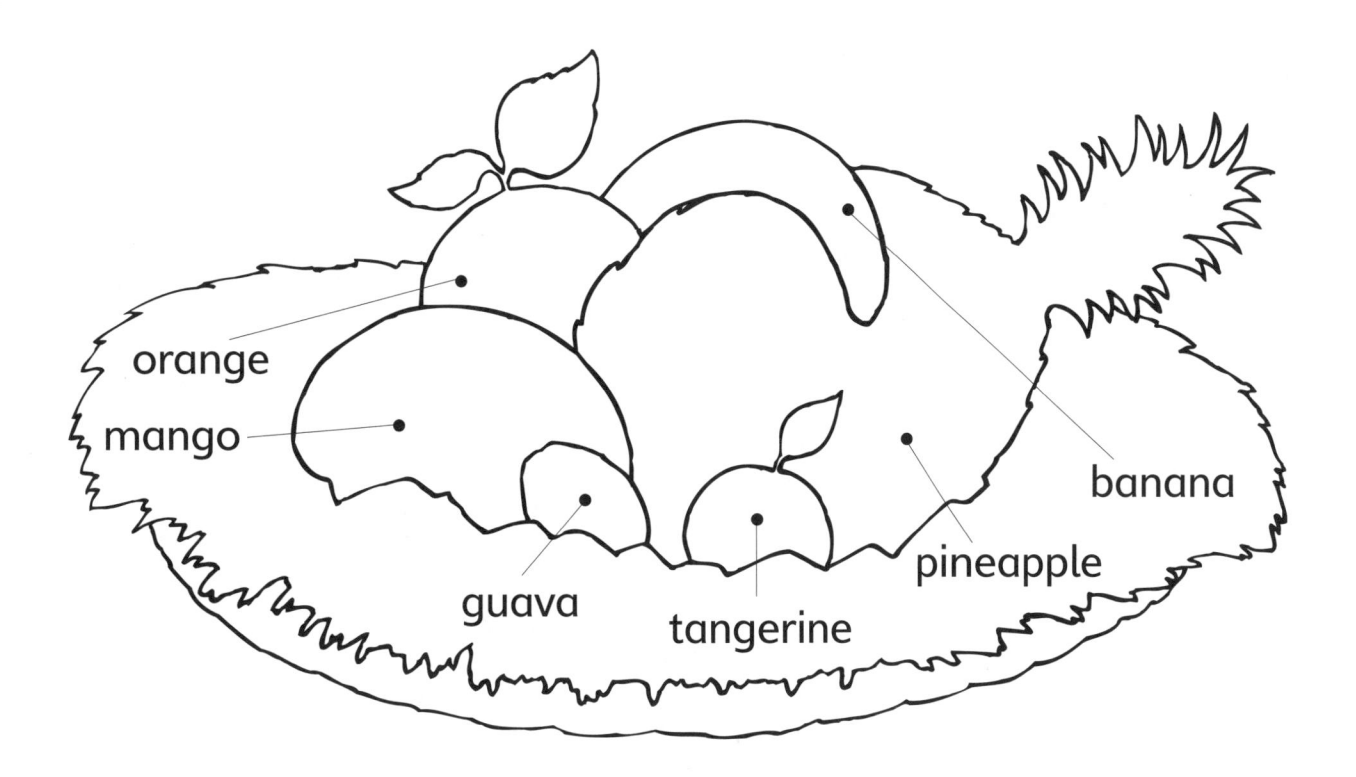

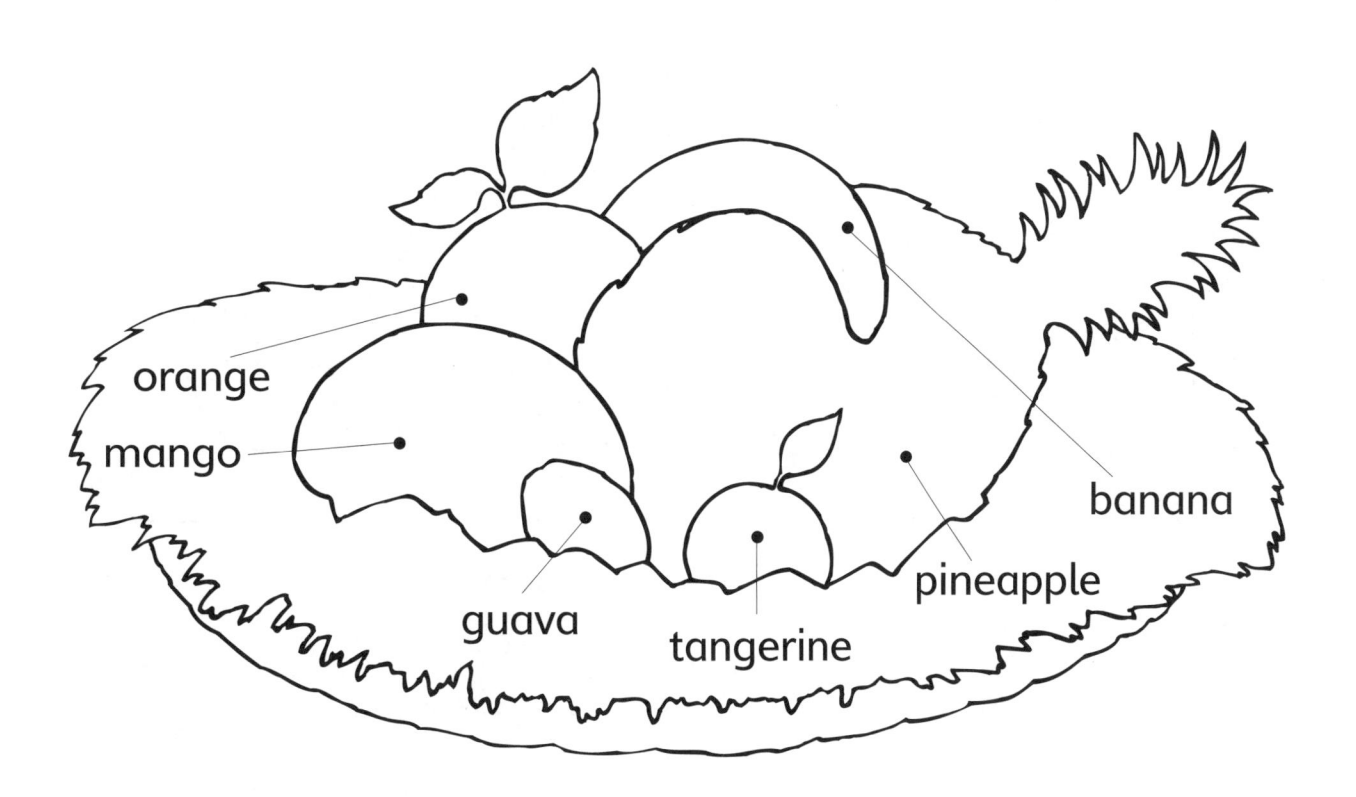

orange
mango
guava
tangerine
pineapple
banana

orange
mango
guava
tangerine
pineapple
banana

Photocopiable — Handa's Surprise

Fruit basket game

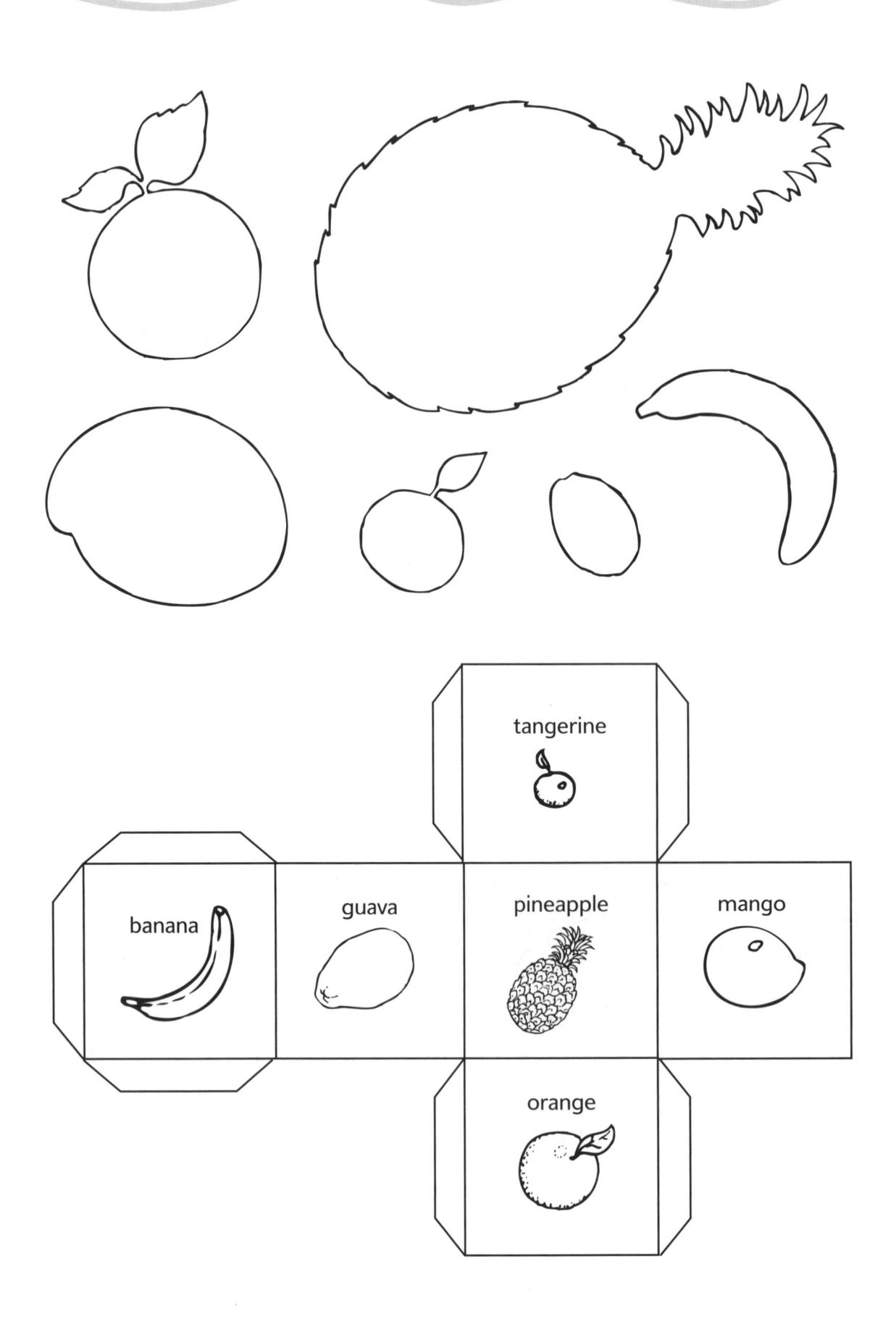

tangerine

banana guava pineapple mango

orange

Handa's Surprise

Photocopiable

African animals

tall and spotted
large-tusked
bright and flighty
black and white striped
cheeky orange
long-necked
curly-horned
clumsy

Village life

Learning intentions
- to discuss the story setting
- to explore village life in Kenya
- to compare rural and urban life in contemporary Africa

Organization
- whole class
- photocopiable page 21 (enlarged and cut)
- a collection of images of everyday life in both urban and rural Africa (you could download images from the *Visit Kenya* Internet site and gather some information on the Luo tribe – see page 32)
- an atlas (or world map)

On a board or a large piece of paper, draw two intersecting circles, large enough to contain all the laminated pictures. Label one 'Town' and the other 'Village'.

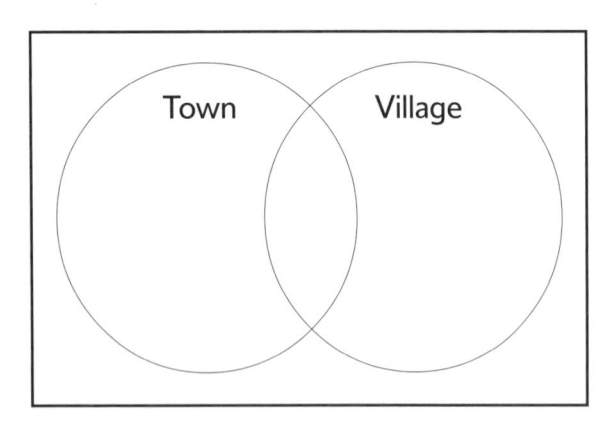

Read the dedication page to the children. Draw attention to the mention of Kenya and the Luo tribe. Discuss the importance of setting in stories – both real and imagined. Turn to the pages near the end of the story that show Handa when she first reaches Akeyo's village. Talk about the picture and draw the children's attention to the drying rack, clay pot and grain store.

Turn back and look at the first two pages which show similar objects in Handa's village. Explain, referring to the map, that many Luo people live in cities like Mombassa and Nairobi, as well as cities in America and Europe, but that the people in the story live on a game reserve.

Introduce the photocopied picture cards and labels. Discuss which of the objects would be found in a city and which in a village. Some may be found in both and so could go in the overlapping area. Stick each image in the correct place with a small piece of Blu-Tack.

Extension
After the whole class activity, ask a small group to sort the pictures again and place them with the correct labels as an independent activity.

Handa's Surprise

Village life

lorry	drying rack	hut	television	clay pot
skyscraper	chicken	grain store	basket of fruit	burger bar

Handa's Surprise

DEVELOPING IDEAS

Puppet play

Learning intentions
- to encourage the oral retelling of the story

Organization
- small group
- photocopiable page 23 (enlarged onto card)
- dowelling rod

Cut out the story characters from the enlarged card photocopy and give each group one or two of the characters to decorate with felt-tipped pens and collage materials. Stick the finished characters onto short pieces of dowelling. Ask the children to retell the story using these stick puppets, improvising thoughts and phrases that could be spoken aloud.

Extension
Develop the children's stories into a puppet play for performance in a plenary session. Vary this by asking a group to produce a shadow play of the story by laying the character outlines flat on an OHP and projecting these images onto the wall. One child could act as the play's narrator.

Another surprise

Learning intentions
- to identify story elements
- to plan story writing

Organization
- whole class
- photocopiable page 24 (enlarged)

Using an enlarged planning sheet in a shared writing activity, map the story elements in Handa's Surprise. 'Character 1' is Handa and 'Character 2' is Akeyo. You will need to simplify the story so that only three pieces of fruit are taken – these will be the 'What 1', 'What 2', and 'What 3'. 'What 4' is the basket filling with tangerines.

On another enlarged planning sheet, plan a similar story with different elements, for example, 'Character 1' could be a boy called Josh, 'Character 2' could be his friend Ayesha. 'Where' might be the walk to school. Ruth packs her bag but loses its contents on the way. She could have paper that blows away ('What 1'), pens that fall out as she jumps over a puddle ('What 2'), crisps that are eaten by the caretaker's dog ('What 3'), and a drink that leaks in her bag ('What 4') – but at least she still has Ayesha's birthday card.

Retell your class story from the completed planning sheet.

Extension
A small group might use their own copy of the story planner to plan a different version.

Handa's Surprise   Read & Respond   Photocopiable

Puppet play

DEVELOPING IDEAS

Photocopiable   Handa's Surprise

Another surprise!

DEVELOPING IDEAS

Character 1	Character 2

Where?

What (1)?	What (2)?
What (3)?	**What (4)?**

Ending

Handa's Surprise

A present for Handa

Learning intentions
- to imagine possible events after the story
- to create empathy with the characters

Organization
- whole class

Tell the children that Akeyo is going to town (Kisii) with her family. She was so pleased with the gift of tangerines that she has saved up her money to buy Handa a present from the market. Ask:

- *What would Handa like?*
  Divide a board or flip chart sheet into two columns. Write the words 'will she like the' above each column and 'or' at the dividing line. Some starting ideas like 'a new pair of flip-flops' or a 'bright sparkling bracelet' could be used.

Extension
Some of these ideas can be developed into the thank-you letter activity described below.

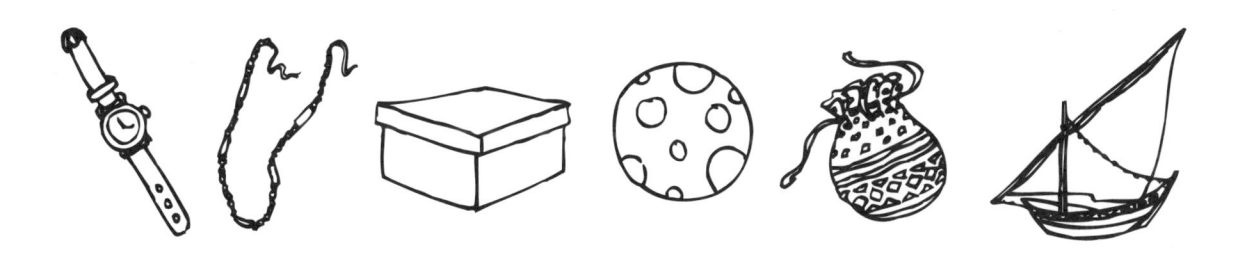

Thank you for the surprise!

Learning intentions
- to extend understanding of the story
- to write in letter form

Organization
- small group
- photocopiable page 26

Give out copies of photocopiable page 26. Explain that there are some rather dangerous animals about, so Akeyo isn't allowed to visit her friend Handa. Instead she will have to write a letter of thanks for the tangerines. She may also want to suggest some plans for the future. Tell the children to write Akeyo's letter to Handa, as if they are Akeyo. Remind them to include the date.

Extension
Some children might take on the role of Handa and write back to Akeyo.

Thank you

DEVELOPING IDEAS

Dear Handa,

Love from
Akeyo

Handa's Surprise

Other animals

Learning intentions
- to look closely at the illustrations
- to develop an appreciation of the story setting

Organization
- whole class
- Big Book version of *Handa's Surprise* (if available)

With the children, look closely at the illustrations and, on a board or large piece of paper, compile a shared list of all the animals that feature in the story. If the children are already very familiar with the story, begin without the book and challenge them to give the names of the animals from memory.

As well as the eight 'character' animals that take fruit from Handa's basket, more appear in the background of the illustrations. With the children, look very carefully at the illustrations and list all the animals and insects they find. Encourage the children to help you to spell the animal names as you add them to the list. (There are about 25 different animals and insects, though the children may not be able to name or distinguish them all.)

Extension
Ask children to sort the words that you have listed into the two categories of 'animal' or 'insect'.

Handa's story

Learning intentions
- to imagine the story told from another point of view
- to develop characterization through role play

Organization
- small group
- 'pretend' microphones (made from cardboard tubes)

Put the children into groups of three. Explain that one person in each group will be the interviewer, one will be Handa and the third will be Akeyo. Provide a microphone for each interviewer and explain that it is their job to think of questions to ask Handa and Akeyo about what happened in the story. For example, questions to Handa:
- *What happened to you today?*
- *What sort of fruit did you put in your basket?*
- *Did the basket begin to feel lighter?*
- *Could you hear anything on your journey?*

Questions for Akeyo might be:
- *Were you expecting Handa?*
- *What had you been doing today?*
- *Will you be visiting Handa soon?*
- *Will you take her a present?*

The children can take turns to try each of the roles so that everyone has a chance to be the interviewer.

Lift the flap

Learning intentions
- to practise the recognition of words which occur frequently in the story
- to recall descriptive vocabulary

Organization
- whole class
- photocopiable page 29 (folded and cut)

Before laminating the photocopied sheet, write the names of the four fruit on the front of each flap (see diagram). Divide the class into two teams. Ask for a volunteer from one team to point to a fruit name.

Invite a member of the other team to read the name of the fruit and then describe it, using familiar words from the text (such as *soft* and *yellow* for the banana). Lift the flap to check the answer.

Once the game has been introduced to the class it can be used as an independent group activity.

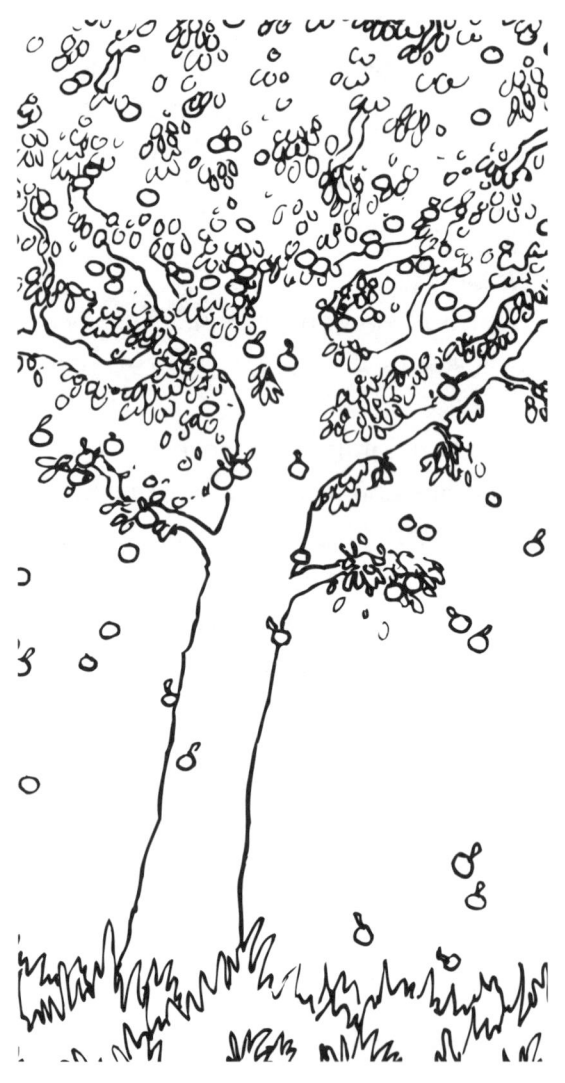

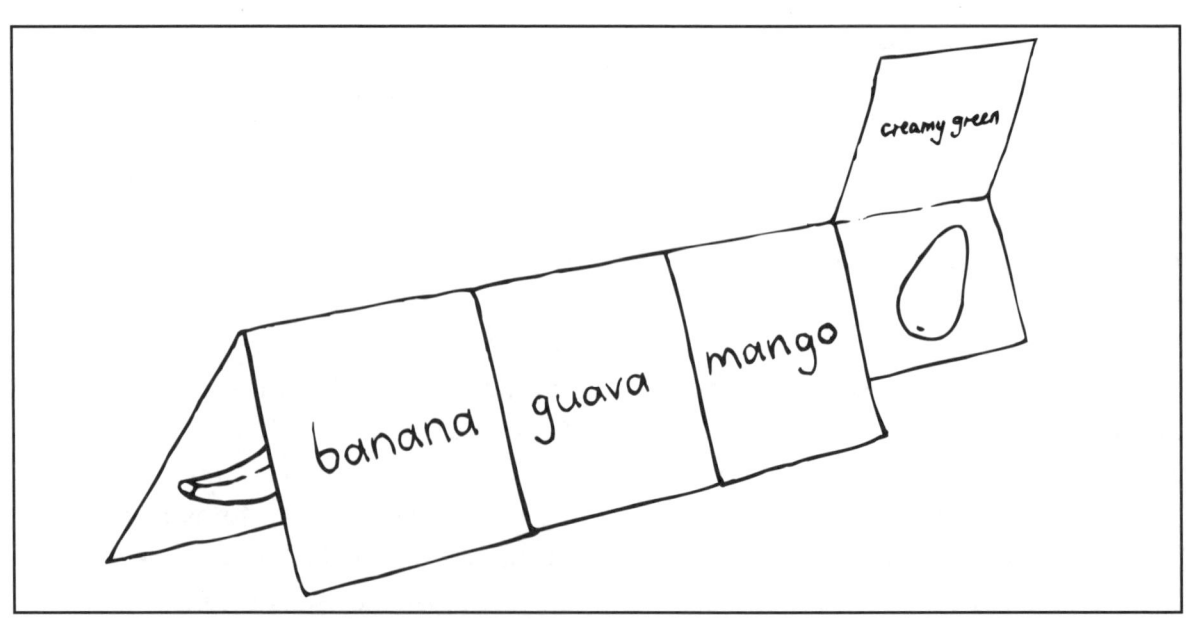

Handa's Surprise

Photocopiable

Lift the flap

creamy green	
ripe red	
sweet-smelling	
soft yellow	

Photocopiable

29

Handa's Surprise

Meeting time

EVALUATION

Learning intentions
- to reflect on events that occur in the story
- to reflect on learning about the story setting

Organization
- whole class
- prepared letter (see below)

Before you begin, prepare a short letter from an official body (such as the Government of Kenya, or Game International) saying that the game reserve is to be closed down. Villagers will be given free housing in a big city (Nairobi) and the animals will be sold off to zoos around the world. The area is to be used for sweetcorn production.

Begin the session by seating the children in a circle. Invite them to take on the roles of different animals and characters in the story. Use the main characters (Handa, Akeyo and the larger animals) but include parents and other villagers too. You could have several children playing the larger animals. Some children may want to be one of the smaller animals or insects.

Ask Handa if she enjoys living in the village and why, ask Akeyo why Handa is a good friend and question some of the animals about their actions in the story. Some of the animals may wish to apologize for frightening Handa or for stealing her fruit. Others may wish to congratulate her for her bravery or kindness. Find out if the animals and insects like living in the game reserve.

Now read out the letter. This is best done if you go into role as an official visitor (putting on a smart jacket or sitting in a different chair can help to signal this to the children). Explain to the children that decisions about the future have already been taken and that they should make ready for the change.

Now come out of role and discuss the children's feelings about the letter and the future developments. After discussing these ask what could be done to change the minds of the officials. Accept all the children's ideas but suggest that you begin by making a poster to express your feelings. Work together to think up an eye-catching image and a short slogan of protest.

Extension
Encourage the children to design their own posters, letters of protest, newspaper or television reports.

Handa's Surprise

USING THIS BOOK

The activities in this book are designed to help develop children's response to stories in the early stages of their literacy development. *Handa's Surprise* is a book that offers many learning opportunities for young children. The story takes place in a different cultural context and is told through predictable and patterned language. The emphasis is on text level work, although a number of the activities provide opportunities for sentence and word level work.

The **Ways in** activity offers ideas for introducing the book to the children. Opportunities are provided for them to consider basic text conventions such as title, author, the use of illustration, dedications and endpapers. It will help children to make informed and critical choices when selecting their own reading material.

The **Making sense** activities draw out the key features of the book. Whole-class activities encourage the children to look closely at the ways in which meaning is communicated through illustration, story structure, patterned language and specific vocabulary choices. The group work allows children to explore these ideas in greater depth.

The **Developing ideas** activities allow children to explore the story in different ways: through oral story-telling, role play, games and creative writing. They aim to develop personal responses and encourage the children to revisit the book and feel confident in their independent reading or retelling of the story.

The **Evaluation** activity encourages children to reflect on the story and its setting. They are asked to consider issues concerning the protection of natural habitats and traditional ways of life.

CLASSROOM MANAGEMENT

These activities can be used across a number of literacy sessions. It is suggested that the book be introduced through the **Ways in** activity, followed by the further reading of the story outlined on page 5. Further sessions could begin with a whole-class activity, followed by groups of children working on related activities, differentiated to meet individual needs.

Multiple copies of *Handa's Surprise* will make classroom organization easier for some of the small-group activities, although a number of these can be completed without direct access to the text. Those activities requiring use of the book are indicated by the 📖 icon.

DIFFERENTIATION

The activities are designed to cover the range of literacy development throughout Key Stage 1 and can be matched to the needs of particular groups of children. A number of the whole-class and group activities can be differentiated by outcome and are suitable for children at different stages of language and literacy development.

LINKING ACTIVITIES

In the **Making sense** section the first four whole-class activities are linked to group activities designed to consolidate or extend the learning intentions. This is

HELP!

Activities	General learning intentions
Reading the story	● plot
Handa's journey	● key events
Telling the tale	● story structure
Handa	● character
What do you think?	● inference
Grasping animals	● illustrations
Will she like it?	● sentence structure and punctuation
Fruit salad	
Vanishing fruit	● vocabulary development
Fruit basket game	● word recognition
African animals	

illustrated in the grid. Whole-class sessions are underlined.

Matching the book to your class
Handa's Surprise enjoys considerable popularity with primary school teachers and pupils as the vibrant artwork of Eileen Browne continues to attract a growing following. The book has a simple story line and its patterned and repetitive structure is supportive to early readers. Through the interplay of visual and verbal text it involves children in characters' points of view in a very natural way. In addition, it introduces children to a culture and a way of life that may be unfamiliar to them and provides a starting point for the exploration of a variety of geographical and social themes.

Handa's Surprise is ideal for reading aloud and can be reread many times without losing its appeal. With growing familiarity, children will enjoy joining in, taking over and reading independently.

The skills grid on the inside back cover of this book outlines the reading strategies, comprehension and response skills developed through the activities. Opportunities are also provided for other learning, including objectives from the National Literacy Strategy and cross-curricular links.

Recommended resources
For all activities it is assumed that the children will have access to writing and drawing materials. In addition, some of the activites will require general art materials and equipment, including glue, scissors and felt-tipped pens.

Further reading by Eileen Browne
Tick Tock (Walker Books)
No Problem (Walker Books)
Where's that Bus? (Walker Books)
Footprints in the Forest: A Chembakolli story [by Taahra Ghazi] (Action Aid)
Through my Window; Wait and See; In a Minute [with Tony Bradman] (Mammoth)
CD-ROM: *Footprints in the Forest* clipart (Action Aid)

Other information
'Wild Animals' chart (Byeway).
www.visit-Kenya.com (maps; slide show and information on game reserves).
www.owlnet.rice.edu (details on the Luo).
www.marketvis.com/gabeplacio/luo.html (images of traditional Luo village huts).
www.blissites.com/Kenya/instruments/shaker.html (how to make a Luo percussion instrument).
En Mana Kuoyo – Ayub Ogada music CD.